BIRDS

By Patricia Lantier-Sampon
Illustrated by Jeff Meyer

Gareth Stevens Publishing
MILWAUKEE

For a free color catalog describing Gareth Stevens' list of high-quality books, call 1-800-341-3569 (USA) or 1-800-461-9120 (Canada).

Library of Congress Cataloging-in-Publication Data

Lantier-Sampon, Patricia.
    Birds / by Patricia Lantier-Sampon; illustrated by Jeff Meyer (Jeffrey D.).
       p. cm. -- (Wings)
    Includes index.
    ISBN 0-8368-0541-0
    1. Birds--Juvenile literature. 2. Birds--Flight--Juvenile literature. [1. Birds. 2. Flight.] I. Meyer, Jeff, ill. II. Title. III. Series: Lantier-Sampon, Patricia — Wings.
    QL676.2.L36   1994
    598--dc20   91-50345

Edited, designed, and produced by
Gareth Stevens Publishing
1555 North RiverCenter Drive, Suite 201
Milwaukee, Wisconsin 53212, USA

Designer: Kristi Ludwig

Printed in the United States of America

1 2 3 4 5 6 7 8 9 99 98 97 96 95 94

Contents

Birds on the wing are a beautiful sight. Their movements can teach us the basics of flight!

Hummingbirds

Hummingbirds hover with delicate poise. Their wings flutter quickly with a soft, humming noise.

Canaries

Canaries sing joyful, melodious songs. Their quivering notes attract people in throngs.

Woodpeckers

Woodpeckers hammer and drum
on tall trees. They lick up small
insects with ravenous ease.

8

Swans

Whistling swans fly south to warm weather. They form V-shaped patterns and migrate together.

Puffins

Puffins are seabirds in bold black-and-white. Their colorful beaks are a comical sight.

Parrots

Amazon parrots are tropical birds. They sport brilliant feathers and repeat silly words.

Owls

Owls can swoop and hunt in the night. Their strange hooting noises often cause quite a fright!

Flamingoes

Flamingoes are waders, some white and some pink.

They bend their long necks
upside-down when they drink.

Penguins

Penguins don't move like most birds you know. They swim in cold waters and slide in the snow.

Eagles

Eagles majestically soar through the sky. Their awesome maneuvers inspire us to fly.

Birds are such noble and fabulous
creatures. Wouldn't *you* like to
have wings?

Glossary

hover: to stay in the same place or to hang with a fluttering motion in the air.

maneuvers: skillful or carefully planned movements.

melodious: having a pleasing sound.

migrate: to move from one place or climate to another.

ravenous: very hungry.

throngs: large groups of people; crowds.

Index